THE CATECHIST'S
FIELD GUIDE

CONFIRMATION

Colin MacIver

ASCENSION

West Chester, Pennsylvania

Ascension
Post Office Box 1990
West Chester, PA 19380
1-800-376-0520
ascensionpress.com

Cover and interior design: Stella Ziegler
Interior art: Mike Moyers
Printed in the United States of America

ISBN 978-1-950784-36-3

"The definitive aim of catechesis is to put people not only in touch but in communion, in intimacy, with Jesus Christ."

(CATECHESI TRADENDAE 5)

CONTENTS

Introduction

Since you have picked up this *Catechist's Field Guide to Confirmation*, you have already said yes to a rather bold endeavor—Confirmation preparation. This is important work as candidates are at a developmental crossroads in so many ways. You have this field guide in your hands because you are involved in the adventure of preparing candidates to receive this powerful sacrament.

In order to be effective at what we set out to accomplish, we need to first identify our objective and align our actions to it. This is true for sports, fitness, nutrition, business, home improvement—or our faith. When we clearly understand our goal, we are far more likely to achieve it. What is the ultimate goal in Confirmation preparation, though? Even as catechists, we might not be able to answer this question precisely.

So let's take a short quiz.

Please identify the goal of Confirmation preparation from among the following options:

☐ To prepare candidates for the honor of attending a special Mass celebrated by a bishop, at which they will be properly attired and well behaved.

☐ To ensure candidates are knowledgeable about Catholic teaching. At the very least, that they know the Creed and the Mass responses, and have some passing acquaintance with the Bible and the *Catechism of the Catholic Church* (CCC).

☐ To help candidates understand the value of attending Mass regularly. Since some candidates and their families do not attend Sunday Mass every week, we want to promote Mass participation as the central activity of the parish.

☐ To prepare candidates for an encounter with Jesus that becomes the foundation of lifelong discipleship, a relationship rooted in their identity as sons and daughters of God—filled with the Holy Spirit and equipped for the mission to which God has called them.

So what did we see here?

The first three goals are fine, but they are not really the point of Confirmation prep. If our focus is on any of them, we might never arrive at the primary goal—"to prepare candidates for an encounter with Jesus." If we start there, however, the other goals will follow.

To be clear, we should ensure that our candidates are prepared for the Confirmation ceremony, and we should work hard to teach them the content of the Faith. We should certainly work hard to get them and their families to attend weekly Mass. We should, however, do all of these things in service of the overall goal—which is to prepare them for what Confirmation actually *does* in their lives: Root them more deeply in their identity as God's sons and daughters and equip them for the mission to which God calls them (see CCC 1303).

This *Catechist's Field Guide to Confirmation* is intended to help you accomplish all of the goals just discussed by setting out on a quest to accomplish the highest goal. We will start this quest by taking a step back and looking at the larger question of what Confirmation actually is and does. From there we will chart a course to building an effective Confirmation preparation experience that addresses the needs of your parish and situation. We will get practical about who and what are involved, with the hope that this *Field Guide* will be both a help in developing your Confirmation preparation program and a quick reference when you are out "in the field" working with candidates (and their parents).

Thank you for your ministry
and your openness to the Holy Spirit!

A CRASH COURSE IN CONFIRMATION

Since we are on a quest for effective Confirmation preparation, let's first look at what Confirmation is and what it does. What exactly are we preparing our candidates to receive? Unfortunately, the purpose of the preparation process is not entirely clear to some catechists, nor is it to many who have already received this sacrament. To many, Confirmation is merely a rite of passage, a "graduation" from formal religious education, an opportunity to make a personal commitment to the Catholic Faith.

... Not exactly.

The mistaken view of Confirmation as "Catholic graduation" is probably rooted in when and how the sacrament is usually received—that is, by teenagers at the "end" of a parish's religious education program. As we have already mentioned, Confirmation has much more to do with discipleship than it does with graduation.

In the second chapter of Acts, we read about the "first Confirmation" at Pentecost. After three years accompanying Jesus during his public ministry, the apostles witnessed his passion, death, resurrection, and ascension. They were gathered together, awaiting the coming of the Spirit as promised by the Lord. They had been assured by Jesus that it was better that he go so that this Advocate, the Holy Spirit, could be sent.

Notice that when the Holy Spirit descends upon the apostles, signified by wind and flame (see Acts 2:2-3), they were not handed diplomas to certify that they had mastered Jesus' teachings. No, they were *filled with the Holy Spirit*, who empowers them to go out and fulfill the mission that Jesus had entrusted to them.

Earlier, in John's Gospel, Jesus had "paved the way"
with his apostles for the coming of the Spirit, saying:

"If you love me, you will keep my commandments.
And I will ask the Father, and he will give you
another Counselor, to be with you forever, even
the Spirit of truth" (JOHN 14:16-17).

"But when the Counselor comes, whom I shall send you from
the Father, even the Spirit of truth, who proceeds from the
Father, he will bear witness to me" (JOHN 15:26).

"It is to your advantage that I go away; for if I do not go away,
the Counselor will not come to you; but if I go, I will send him to
you. And when he comes, he will convince the world of sin and
of righteousness and of judgment" (JOHN 16:7-8).

The Holy Spirit, the Counselor, is a divine Person, who "proceeds from the Father and the Son," as we proclaim in the Creed. We first receive the Spirit at Baptism, and then are "sealed" by the Spirit in a special way in Confirmation, which is the "completion of baptismal grace" (CCC 1285).

Why does Jesus speak to his disciples of the "advantage" of the Spirit's coming? Isn't Jesus enough? Because the Holy Spirit lives within us, through grace. There is an even deeper intimacy with God through the Holy Spirit than there would have been sitting by the campfire with Jesus. Jesus himself said so.

So how does the Holy Spirit come to us at Confirmation? What does this sacrament actually accomplish?

Whenever St. Thomas Aquinas sought to make a doctrine or thought clear, he grouped things into threes.

So here are the <u>three</u> essential things to know about Confirmation:

 It is a sacrament.

 It completes Baptism.

 It empowers us for our mission and vocation.

CONFIRMATION
IS A SACRAMENT

An obvious statement, perhaps, but it is worth taking a moment to consider this. We know that a sacrament is *not* a symbolic rite of passage or merely words and gestures we do to mark something spiritual. No, sacraments are *real encounters with Jesus Christ* that actually do something—they give us God's grace. They communicate God's own life into the deepest parts of our beings. Baptism and Confirmation change our souls in a permanent way; they leave an "indelible mark" that empowers us as Christians. (A bold claim, no?) Once baptized and confirmed, always baptized and confirmed.

Keeping to a list of three, we can say that the sacrament of Confirmation:

○ **Is an outward sign ...**

In Confirmation, this sign includes the words spoken by the bishop and the sealing with oil on the candidate's forehead.

· · · · · · · · · · ·

"Jesus breathed on them, and said to them, 'Receive the Holy Spirit!'"

(JOHN 20:22).

· · · · · · · · · · ·

ɸ **... that Jesus entrusted to the Church ...**

From the earliest times the apostles and their successors laid hands and anointed with oil to pass on the gift of the Holy Spirit.

"And Paul ... laid hands on them"

(ACTS 19:6)

· · · · · · · · · · ·

ɸ **... to give grace.**

The gift of God's life poured out into those who receive Confirmation in a way that deepens identity as God's children and equips for the mission of Christian discipleship.

CONFIRMATION
"COMPLETES" BAPTISM

While Baptism is the first step in Christian initiation, Confirmation deepens, matures, and activates a disciple's walk with Christ. The *Catechism* describes exactly what this looks like, and we summarize paragraph 1303 here:

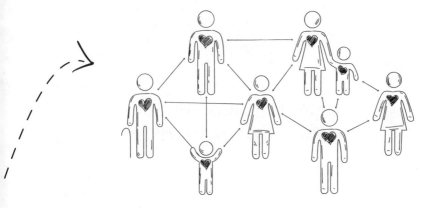

1. Confirmation roots us more deeply in our baptismal identity as sons and daughters so that we can cry out to God as Father (see Romans 8:15).

2. Confirmation brings us closer to Christ.

3. While the gifts of the Holy Spirit are given at Baptism to some degree, they are poured out and increased in Confirmation.

4. In Baptism, we are brought into the Church, the family of God. Confirmation makes our bond with the Church more perfect.

5. We are given a call to missionary discipleship at Baptism. Confirmation, through the Holy Spirit, gives us the strength to be bold witnesses to our Catholic Faith.

CONFIRMATION EQUIPS US FOR
MISSION AND VOCATION

Confirmation, then, roots us in our identity as disciples of Christ—and gives us the strength to live out the Christian life. We can see what this looks like by considering Pentecost (see Acts 2). After receiving the Holy Spirit, the apostles immediately begin living out their mission to preach the gospel. (In fact, the mission of the Church, both then and now, is only possible due to the working of the Spirit in the hearts and souls of its members.) The sacrament of Confirmation is an outpouring of the same Spirit, who calls us to the same mission.

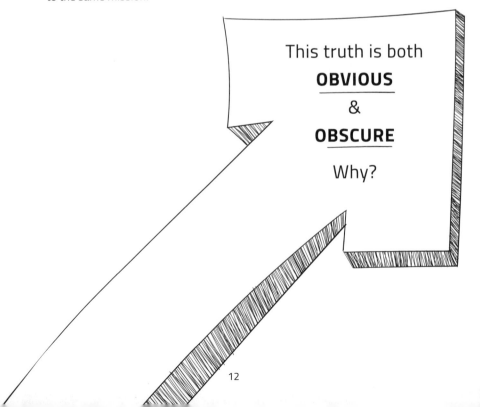

This truth is both

OBVIOUS

&

OBSCURE

Why?

obvious   ⟶

It is **obvious** because most of us would pick Pentecost as the corresponding event in the Bible for Confirmation. Pentecost launched an epic mission.

It is **obvious** because the signs and words of the Confirmation rite are clearly about the mission of Christian life.

It is **obvious** because the gifts of the Holy Spirit, which are clearly connected to the sacraments, are connected to effective Christian discipleship.

obscure   ⟶

It is **obscure** because we may not immediately see the newly confirmed becoming immediately engaged and invested in the mission of the Church.

It may also be **obscure** because the grace God gives us is not flashy, magical, or automatic. Grace works more like a Crock-Pot than a microwave—that is, it works slowly and deliberately so as to yield a better result. (Would you rather a frozen dinner zapped for two minutes or a slow-cooked, Crock-Pot masterpiece?)

It may be **obscure** because the gifts given in Confirmation require cultivation, cooperation, and nourishment through prayer and reception of the other sacraments, especially the Eucharist. Sometimes, these gifts are immediately evident, felt, and experienced. Typically, though, they sprout when the soil is tilled, watered, and weeded. Remember Jesus' parable of the Sower (see Mark 4: 4-9). It is clear that God's grace builds on and works through our cooperation.

Speaking of mission, we associate
the particular gifts (see Isaiah 11) and
fruits of the Holy Spirit (see Galatians
5:22-23) with Confirmation. The gifts
of the Spirit are the necessary equipment
for living as missionary disciples of Jesus,
whereas the Spirit's fruits are the "overflow" and
"afterglow" of his continuous indwelling in our souls.
Rooted in an intimate relationship with God, we
cannot help but be motivated and equipped for
missionary discipleship. When Jesus promised an
advocate who would guide us in all truth (see
John 16:3), he pointed to what the Holy Spirit
would do for our minds and hearts.

THE SEVEN GIFTS OF THE HOLY SPIRIT

St. Thomas Aquinas tells us that the first four gifts of the Spirit—**wisdom, understanding, counsel,** and **knowledge**—are related to our reasoning, while the other three—**fortitude, piety,** and **fear of the Lord**—are related to our appetites and desires. St. Thomas also tells us that while some gifts form our inner life, others relate to how we respond in concrete situations. To keep it simple, think of it this way: all of these gifts, flowing from the Holy Spirit within us, help us to be our truest and freest selves. They give us the "superpowers" we need for what is literally a supernatural mission.

Let's take a look at each gift ...

The gift of **WISDOM** empowers us to see the world in harmony with God's plan, in a way that points our hearts toward heaven.

Practically speaking ...

Wisdom keeps us fixed on heaven as our ultimate goal.

Wisdom helps us make well-discerned decisions with the "big picture" always in mind.

Wisdom prevents us from making judgments that are at odds with God's plan.

Wisdom connects us to the mind of God.

WISDOM

Wisdom makes us aware of the long-term consequences of a potential decision or action— both on earth and in relationship to eternity.

Wisdom helps us see into the hearts of others.

Wisdom shows us how things fit together.

The gift of **KNOWLEDGE** helps us to see things from God's perspective. It allows us to see created things with his mind and act in a way that is pleasing to him.

Practically speaking ...

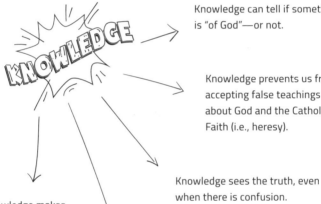

Knowledge can tell if something is "of God"—or not.

Knowledge prevents us from accepting false teachings about God and the Catholic Faith (i.e., heresy).

Knowledge sees the truth, even when there is confusion.

Knowledge makes us quick studies of Catholic doctrine—and helps us communicate these teachings in a way others can understand.

Knowledge helps us to put the things that God made at his service.

The gift of **UNDERSTANDING** helps us to comprehend the meaning of the Word of God and the teachings of the Church. When we grow in understanding, we can act with the gift of counsel (more to come on that ...).

Practically speaking ...

Understanding causes things to "click." (You know, those "ah ha!" moments.)

Understanding helps us comprehend the meaning of Sacred Scripture.

UNDERSTANDING

Understanding allows us to apply our knowledge of Scripture and Church teaching to everyday situations.

Understanding prepares us to be able to teach others.

Understanding helps us grasp the teachings of the Church.

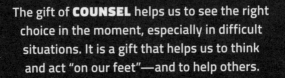

The gift of **COUNSEL** helps us to see the right choice in the moment, especially in difficult situations. It is a gift that helps us to think and act "on our feet"—and to help others.

Practically speaking ...

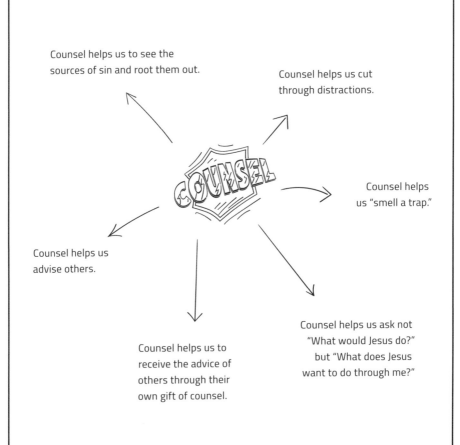

Counsel helps us to see the sources of sin and root them out.

Counsel helps us cut through distractions.

Counsel helps us "smell a trap."

Counsel helps us advise others.

Counsel helps us to receive the advice of others through their own gift of counsel.

Counsel helps us ask not "What would Jesus do?" but "What does Jesus want to do through me?"

The gift of **FORTITUDE** strengthens and grounds our will
as a child of God so that we can overcome—and persevere
in overcoming—our fears. "You have not received a spirit
of slavery to fall back into fear" (Romans 8:15). Fortitude
helps us put into action what counsel makes clear.

Practically speaking ...

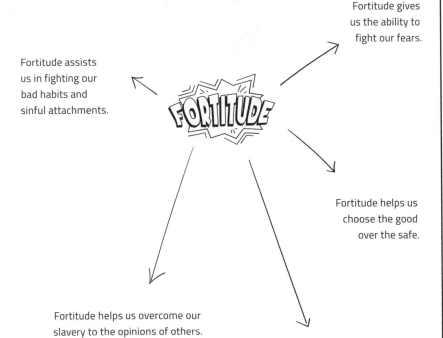

Fortitude gives
us the ability to
fight our fears.

Fortitude assists
us in fighting our
bad habits and
sinful attachments.

Fortitude helps us
choose the good
over the safe.

Fortitude helps us overcome our
slavery to the opinions of others.

Fortitude helps us
overcome anxiety.

The gift of **PIETY** enables us to respect God as our loving Father and to act as his secure, beloved child. "When we cry, 'Abba! Father!' it is the Spirit himself bearing witness ... that we are children of God" (Romans 8:15-16). Piety does not mean simply "following the rules" but acting as a son or daughter of God. Probably the best example of piety in the Bible is Jesus crying out from the Cross to his Father, who had the power to save him (see Hebrews 5:7). Piety is found in Jesus' willingness to learn to obey the Father's will through what he had to suffer (see Hebrews 5:8) to bring us who obey him to salvation.

Practically speaking ...

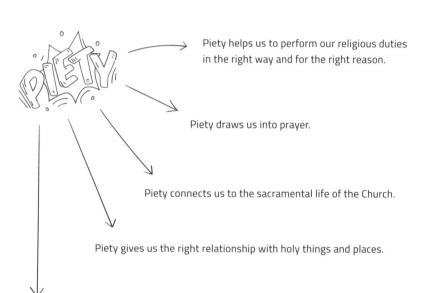

Piety helps us to perform our religious duties in the right way and for the right reason.

Piety draws us into prayer.

Piety connects us to the sacramental life of the Church.

Piety gives us the right relationship with holy things and places.

Piety helps us see God in others—and treat them with love and respect.

The gift of **FEAR OF THE LORD** does not involve being "scared" of God. This gift is sometimes referred to as *reverence*. It helps us to revere God's power and majesty, and it is balanced by piety, which invites us into relationship with him. Think of Moses' encounter with God in the burning bush. When he realizes it is the Lord himself speaking to him, he is so in awe that he covers his face to avoid looking at God's glory (see Exodus 3:1-5). We see this also in the prophet Isaiah's glorious vision of God sitting on a throne with angels flying around him. Isaiah feels so unworthy to be in the divine presence that he responds, "Woe is me, I am ruined!" (see Isaiah 6:1-6).

Practically speaking ...

Fear of the Lord helps us to be in awe of God's power and might.

Fear of the Lord helps us to be aware of our humanity and mortality.

FEAR OF THE LORD

Fear of the Lord moves us to wonder at the power of God in creation (e.g., birth, sunrises and sunsets, rainbows, volcanoes, whales, the universe, etc.).

Fear of the Lord helps us to have a proper respect for the sacraments.

Fear of the Lord prevents us from presuming on God's mercy.

The 12 FRUITS of the HOLY SPIRIT

Along with the gifts of the Holy Spirit, the fruits of the Spirit are related to our identity and mission as disciples of Christ. They are direct effects of the interior dwelling of the Spirit. As Jesus tells his disciples in the Sermon on the Mount, "Every sound tree bears good fruit ... a sound tree cannot bear evil fruit, nor can a bad tree bear good fruit ... Thus you will know them by their fruits" (Matthew 7:17-20).

In their life, a person filled with the Holy Spirit shows the fruits of ...

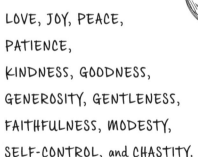

LOVE, JOY, PEACE,
PATIENCE,
KINDNESS, GOODNESS,
GENEROSITY, GENTLENESS,
FAITHFULNESS, MODESTY,
SELF-CONTROL, and CHASTITY.

LOVE

A person filled with the Spirit sees others with God's eyes, takes delight in others, and acts sacrificially for their well-being (even with one who acts like an enemy). The primary example of love is Jesus himself, who gives up his own life for his friends—us (see John 15:13).

JOY

A person filled with the Spirit has a kind of interior smile, a "flowing out of the heart" kind of "zip," regardless of the circumstances. Joy is a contentment of the heart that is obvious and contagious. This is a joy that Jesus alone can give through the Spirit (see John 15:11).

PEACE

A person filled with the Spirit radiates the peace that the world cannot give (see John 14:27). This means that he is composed and balanced within—and seeks to be a peacemaker in the midst of conflicts and divisions (see Matthew 5:9).

PATIENCE

A person filled with the Spirit waits on "God's time" rather than his own. He has confidence in God's providence, trusting that the Lord knows what is best. He is steady and calm, never acting rashly. Patience is also a gift present in the ability to forgive another just as Christ has forgiven us (see Colossians 3:12-14).

KINDNESS

A person filled with the Spirit is more than simply "nice" (which can actually serve our own self-interest by seeking to avoid conflicts or hurt feelings, or to make ourselves look good). The fruit of kindness involves looking out for the true, best interests of others. Kindness allows one to forgive—and even to wish those who have wronged him well (see Colossians 3:12-14).

GOODNESS

A person filled with the Spirit is motivated by what is morally good rather than self-interest. He has a powerful moral compass which he faithfully follows. He lives in light rather than darkness, staying away from bad influences and attaching himself to good ones (see Ephesians 5:3-13).

GENEROSITY

A person filled with the Spirit gives to others out of the blessings he has received from God, recognizing that everything is a gift. He has a heart always open to helping others in need, giving his time, talent, and treasure.

GENTLENESS

A person filled with the Spirit has the right kind of "touch" and handles people and situations with a "delicate reverence." Others feel loved, cared for, and appreciated.

FAITHFULNESS

A person filled with the Spirit is not distracted by challenges or suffering but is steady in his commitment to God and his will. He also fulfills the promises he has made to others (see James 2:12-14).

MODESTY

A person filled with the Spirit dresses and acts appropriately, in a way that protects his human dignity and sexuality.

SELF-CONTROL

A person filled with the Spirit has his impulses in check. When the inner fire of his temper is stoked or when desires are strong, he slows down and brings his emotions into harmony with what is true and good.

CHASTITY

A person filled with the Spirit acts with purity in his or her thoughts, looks, and actions. This fruit flows directly from those of modesty and self-control.

FIVE

REASONS

WHY TEENS
(and their parents)

THEY ARE

BEING

CONFIRMED

GOOD NEWS!

The Confirmation candidates of your parish have been successfully enrolled in your prep program, and they are heading your way for the first session.

But ... do they know why?

As you might suspect, many—if not most—are not seeking to be confirmed out of an ardent desire to become filled with the Holy Spirit and be empowered in their discipleship. No, they are coming because their parents signed them up.

But ... do their PARENTS know why?

It will come as no shock that many of these parents do not attend Mass regularly and are not particularly active in their practice of their faith.

It would be great to report that most candidates show up to Confirmation prep because they are already deeply committed to growing as missionary disciples of Jesus Christ. While some candidates and their parents have such a commitment, most fall somewhere on a continuum of "cultural Catholicism"—they know and believe (some of) the Church's teachings, and attend Mass at least occasionally. Most probably have a limited understanding of the Catholic Faith, in general, and Confirmation, in particular.

Still ... they signed their teens up for Confirmation prep. Even their misconceptions can be a starting point for a fuller understanding and a more effective preparation. Rather than rolling our eyes and lamenting the parent who tells their son or daughter that they have to go through the program to be married in the Church someday, or the parent who insists that their child "graduate" from religious education, we can fan the spark of faith that got them in the door until it becomes a white hot flame.

Let's examine some of the mistaken reasons candidates end up in your program and present some ways to move them toward the real goal of Confirmation.

Confirmation allows young people to make their own commitment to the Catholic Faith. At Baptism, their parents did this for them, but now they affirm the Faith as their own.

What is "off" here?

This reduces the sacrament to a "rite of passage" for teens; it misses entirely what Confirmation actually is and does. Confirmation roots us in our identity as God's sons and daughters and empowers us for a mission of discipleship. In the Eastern rites of the Church, this sacrament is received as an infant during Baptism (along with the Eucharist)—in other words, all of the sacraments of initiation are received together. So a candidate's personal commitment to the Faith cannot be the central purpose of Confirmation.

What is "on" here?

In the Roman rite of the Church, we wait to confer this sacrament until a child has passed the age of reason, usually by several years, and after he or she has received first Eucharist. It seems fitting that a candidate be well disposed and well prepared to be confirmed. So you should not discount the importance of your candidates making a free decision for Christ and the Church. Grace builds on nature, and the power of Confirmation is integrated into the candidate's mind and heart based on this decision.

How can we build from here?

This view is not difficult to build on. In fact, it is not a bad idea to emphasize to candidates that Confirmation preparation gives them an opportunity to make a personal commitment to Christ and the Catholic Faith. Then, show them how this decision makes room for the Holy Spirit to root them more deeply in being a disciple of Christ and empower them for their mission in the Church.

REASON
2

One needs to have received Confirmation to be married in the Church.

What is "off" here?

It is true that Confirmation, which completes our Christian initiation, is normally required for the sacrament of Matrimony. The problem here is if one seeks to be confirmed *only* (or even mainly) because he or she wants a Church wedding someday. Since this is often seen as culturally important or in continuity with family tradition, one is merely planning ahead. This can turn Confirmation into a hoop one simply needs to jump through. This misses the power and nature of both Confirmation and Matrimony, neither of which can be reduced to rites of passage, cultural icons, or photo ops.

What is "on" here?

Since Confirmation strengthens us in our identity as Christians and equips us for our mission as disciples, it does have a strong relationship to the sacrament of Matrimony. It takes the grace of the Spirit to live out the vocation of marriage (as it does any vocation). What makes great marriages and strong families? Certainly the gifts of the Spirit: wisdom, counsel, understanding, piety, knowledge, courage, and fear of the Lord.

How can we build from here?

Understanding that this is the starting point for some candidates and their parents, we can build toward the idea that both marriage and Confirmation are sacraments—that is, they are encounters with Christ that give grace and transform us. Confirmation lays the foundation for being a good spouse (or a holy priest, consecrated religious, or blessed single person). Focus on presenting a deeper understanding of both sacraments and help candidates move beyond seeing them as cultural moments or Church requirements to appreciating them as celebrations of relationship.

REASON

3

To be a godparent at Baptism, you need to be confirmed.

What is "off" here?

For some, the primary motivation to be confirmed is so that they can one day be a godparent to a niece, nephew, etc. They see being a godparent as a sign of honor and understand that being confirmed is a prerequisite. Again, such a focus can reduce the sacraments of Baptism and Confirmation to merely ceremonial and honorific events rather than identity and mission.

What is "on" here?

The desire to pass on something to future nieces and nephews acknowledges that there is something to pass on. If a candidate is concerned about one day being a godparent, there is at least some sense that the Faith should be handed on to the next generation. This ties into the mission given to us by Jesus: "Go ... and make disciples" (Matthew 28:19).

How can we build from here?

Here, we have an opportunity to present the relationship between Baptism and Confirmation and expand the candidates' understanding of what each sacrament is and does. In addition, discuss the actual role of a godparent, as well as a Confirmation sponsor, both of which require being a role model and mentor in the Faith. (Such a discussion might influence a candidate's sponsor choice—and the desire to someday be a godparent is a spark that can be blown into flame.)

REASON

4

Confirmation is just graduation from religious education.

What is "off" here?

Confirmation is *not* religious ed graduation. It is not a diploma that certifies mastery of Christian teaching, nor is it a ceremony to mark the end of learning about the Faith. Unfortunately, this view of Confirmation is common—and does seem to come to pass in many parishes.

What is "on" here?

Obviously, preparing candidates for Confirmation is a priority of every religious education program. The point of presenting the content of the Catholic Faith is to ensure that candidates are well disposed to receive the sacrament and know what it does. During the Confirmation ceremony, the pastor certifies to the bishop that the candidates are well prepared to be confirmed.

The idea that Confirmation is "graduation" is true *only in this aspect:* One is confirmed only after he or she has been fully prepared. The problem is that this attitude misses the core reality of Confirmation—receiving an outpouring of the Holy Spirit that leads one deeper into the life of the Church, not away from it.

How can we build from here?

Start by calling out this fairly common misunderstanding. Then, move on and explain that religious education is about more than just handing on facts; it is about preparing for an outpouring of the Holy Spirit so that candidates can be fully invested in the life of the Church. The point is to move into a deeper relationship with God and the Church.

REASON

5

You get confirmed to make your parents (and grandparents) happy.

What is "off" here?

Sigh ... where do we start?

What is "on" here?

It is certainly honorable to want one's parents and grandparents to be happy. While this is a flawed motivation to seek Confirmation, it might indicate a sense of duty and respect for family in a candidate that could spark into a flame if it is "fanned" correctly.

How can we build from here?

Start from square one. Take a deep breath, pray a Hail Mary, and skip to the next section of this *Field Guide*.

Go ahead and turn the page ...

The

Stages
of an Effective
Confirmation Experience

The following stages are adapted from the ancient, tried and true method of preparation for *catechumens*—those who were preparing to be baptized—in the early Church. The catechumenate, both then and now, is a preparation for full initiation into the Church at the Easter Vigil. During this sacred Liturgy, those who have been preparing to enter into the Church receive the sacraments of Baptism, Confirmation, and Holy Eucharist.

These stages represent a logical flow that aims to prepare one for full initiation into the Church. Since each stage seeks to form a catechumen's mind and heart for authentic Christian discipleship, each is also helpful for catechists preparing candidates for Confirmation. (Note that the Church's *General Directory for Catechesis* presents this flow as the model for all catechesis.)

These five stages, which can be reflected in how you set up your overall program, should be considered each time you meet with your candidates. Each session should seek to be a relevant encounter with Christ and his teachings that empowers candidates for real-life discipleship beyond their reception of Confirmation.

Here is an overview of the five stages, adapted
for Confirmation prep:

1 PRE-EVANGELIZATION

Preparation starts by establishing relevance, trust,
and understanding.

2 EVANGELIZATION

It then moves on to a proclamation of Jesus and
the gospel.

3 CATECHESIS

Then, after there is a movement and commitment of
the heart, the content of the Faith is presented.

4 PURIFICATION AND ENLIGHTENMENT

This is an apprenticeship in living as a disciple
of Christ.

5 MYSTAGOGY

"Learning about the mysteries," continuing to
grow in learning, prayer, and discipleship.

PRE-EVANGELIZATION

What This Is

Pre-evangelization refers to what must happen to share the Faith effectively with an audience. Everyone naturally seeks truth, goodness, and beauty. We also seek authenticity and community, and we long for something that can address our hurts, anxieties, and need for meaning.

This stage is where we meet people where they are, addressing what they really care about. We also help them to understand themselves better. Here, we show understanding and genuine care and seek to establish credibility and trust.

What This Looks Like in Confirmation Preparation

In Confirmation preparation, this is where the catechist is challenged to put on a proverbial stethoscope and listen with the ear of the heart. To a catechist who is concerned about "covering all the material," this might seem like a waste of time ... but it is not. Skipping this step is like forgetting to open a container before pouring something into it.

Make sure you ...

- Know the name of each candidate.
- "Waste" five minutes every session on informal conversation.
- Check in with your candidates on their state of mind and well-being.
- Discover their interests.
- Pray for them.
- Put yourself in their shoes.

- Meet them "where they are."

- Understand (as much as possible) their culture and what is important to them.

- Consider how different things are now from when you were their age.

- Note that bad behaviors are often signs of big hurts.

- Ask questions and listen without making judgment.

- Start with safe questions and build out into deeper questions.

Stage

2

EVANGELIZATION

What This Is

Evangelization means the actual sharing of the gospel message. This involves handing on the *kerygma*, the proclamation of the core message of the Good News—namely, Jesus.

Here is the tricky thing. When St. Paul arrived in Corinth, people had not yet heard this news. After he preached, the Corinthians might have been intrigued because his message sounded a bit crazy—God became man, died, rose, ascended to heaven, then sent the Holy Spirit and handed over the whole enterprise to some fishermen from the sticks and a tentmaker (Paul). St. Paul sure had a pretty interesting hook.

Today, though, nearly everyone has heard this news—or thinks they have. They may also have heard counterfeit, half-baked, or even downright heretical versions of the Christian message, which muddies the water even more. So now when we share the words of Jesus, people's eyes tend to glaze over and the walls come up. It all sounds like something they have heard before.

What St. Paul offered was not just a story about something that happened in the past; it was an encounter with the living Jesus.

So many today who claim *Catholic* as their religious preference have not quite had the core experience of the Catholic Faith, which is a life-changing encounter with Jesus. Without a relationship with Christ, the rest seems boring and irrelevant. Who cares about sacraments if they don't first care about the God who loves them and sent his Son to die for their sins?

What This Looks Like in Confirmation Preparation

Since we cannot assume that our candidates have truly been evangelized, our goal must be to draw them into an experience of the living Jesus. If we do not succeed, they will not care about anything else we have to say.

This means that the catechist has to be a witness as well as a teacher. Here are some practical tips:

- Remember to evangelize (and "re-evangelize") at every session.
- Practice articulating the *kerygma*, something like this:
  - » We were created with a purpose.
  - » We are broken by sin.
  - » We have been redeemed by God, through the Cross of Christ.
  - » We are called to conversion.
  - » We are called to a relationship with Jesus.
  - » We are invited into the life of the Church.
- Share your own faith and talk about what God is doing in your life.
- Pray to the Holy Spirit before, during, and after each session.
- Relate whatever you are teaching to the *kerygma*.

CATECHESIS

What This Is

Catechesis seeks to mature the seed of faith planted in evangelization by handing on the content of Catholic teaching, which flows from the *kerygma*. Catechesis answers the many questions that follow from an initial encounter with Christ and educates those who seek true discipleship. Growing in their knowledge of the Catholic Faith helps put candidates into deeper communion with Jesus.

What This Looks Like in Confirmation Preparation

Here, the aim of catechesis is to ensure candidates have a broad knowledge of the Catholic Faith, with a particular emphasis on the Holy Spirit and the sacrament of Confirmation. This Catholic literacy, though, must be continually connected to the person of Jesus. Abstract, disconnected facts will not do.

Offer a "big picture" review and presentation of the fundamentals of the Faith, including presentations on ...

- The **real presence of Jesus in the Eucharist** that invites candidates into the Mass as full, conscious, and active participants.

- The **sacrament of Reconciliation** that includes opportunities to receive it.

- **Mary** and the **communion of saints**.

- The **Holy Spirit** and the **Spirit's role in Confirmation**.

- The actual **Confirmation rite**, one that drives home that "as we pray, so we believe." *(The Confirmation Liturgy is loaded with teaching opportunities.)*

- **Life in Christ** and what this looks like in practical terms. *(Start with the basics, then move on to the more difficult teachings of the Church on chastity and social issues.)*

- **Catholic social teaching**, focusing on how this translates into experiences of service.

- The vocation that Confirmation will prepare the candidate for.

Stage 4

PURIFICATION AND ENLIGHTENMENT

What This Is

This is the stage that prepares candidates for the daily practice of the Christian life, including developing the practice of prayer. It also seeks to assist in the deepening of living an integrated experience of discipleship. It seeks to answer such questions as: How does a committed Christian interact with the world? How do we grow in virtue? How are the gifts of the Holy Spirit developed and integrated beyond Confirmation?

Here the catechist serves as a mentor and should encourage an ongoing one-on-one interaction between the candidate and his or her sponsor. This stage is intensive and intentional. For those in RCIA, this takes place during Lent, so it is accompanied by an entire season of prayer, fasting, and almsgiving.

What This Looks Like in Confirmation Preparation

- Mentor your candidates through prayer. Pray with them, using various prayers, methods, and approaches.

- Invite your candidates to ask questions about living as a committed Catholic in the world.

- Develop a concrete plan to bring sponsors into the process. (For sponsors who live out of the area, have them join your sessions via online video conferencing.)

- Encourage each candidate to select a confirmed and practicing Catholic as his or her sponsor. This should be someone who takes their faith seriously and with whom he or she can have a real conversation. (Discourage candidates from choosing their favorite aunt, uncle, or cousin—unless he or she is a good role model in the Faith.)

- Continue encouraging regular reception of the sacrament of Reconciliation.

- If any candidates are not attending Sunday Mass every week, strongly encourage them to do so.

- Continue providing opportunities for service to the poor, vulnerable, and marginalized.

Stage
5

MYSTAGOGY

What This Is

The stage of *mystagogy*, a Greek word meaning "learning about the mysteries," follows the initiation of the believer into the Church at Easter and continues until Pentecost. It is a process of growing in the Faith through prayer, learning, and practicing with other believers. Here, the fully initiated "stretch their sacramental legs," see the world with "confirmed vision," and move more deeply into the life of the Church.

This fifth stage is often news to many parishes, so they have no established plan or tradition for implementing it. The first four stages logically form the typical flow of preparation for Confirmation, but the need for *mystagogy*—for helping the newly confirmed continue to grow in their discipleship with Jesus—is often overlooked. There is no formal follow up, no sense that the program has been building up to a new and heightened presence in the life of the Church.

With this in mind, things can be put into place to ensure your newly confirmed can become full, conscious, active participants in the life of the Church—in other words, disciples. Here are some ideas for practical *mystagogy* beyond Confirmation:

- Offer a teen-oriented study or program immediately after Confirmation so the group can continue to grow in their understanding of the Faith together and stay active in the parish.

- Coordinate with your parish youth ministry and help candidates plug into the opportunities currently available.

- Encourage your newly confirmed to consider more active participation in parish ministry, perhaps as lectors, ushers, service volunteers, junior Confirmation team members, etc.

- Start planting the seeds earlier in your Confirmation prep program: "After you are confirmed, you will ..."

- Consider having a reunion or social event for all the newly confirmed, perhaps six months or so after they have received the sacrament.

The People in Your
Confirmation Neighborhood

THE FOUR "TYPES" OF CANDIDATES IN YOUR PROGRAM

Each of your candidates is a unique and unrepeatable masterpiece of God. That being said, there are certain "types" of candidates, each with different experiences, characteristics, motivations, and attitudes, that tend to be found in every parish Confirmation prep program. Here are a few candidate profiles that might be helpful to consider as you develop an approach to mentoring and forming your candidates on their journey toward Confirmation.

Note: *The following profiles are provided only to help you respond effectively when ministering to candidates with particular attitudes, backgrounds, and behaviors. As catechists, we always want to avoid "labeling" our students.*

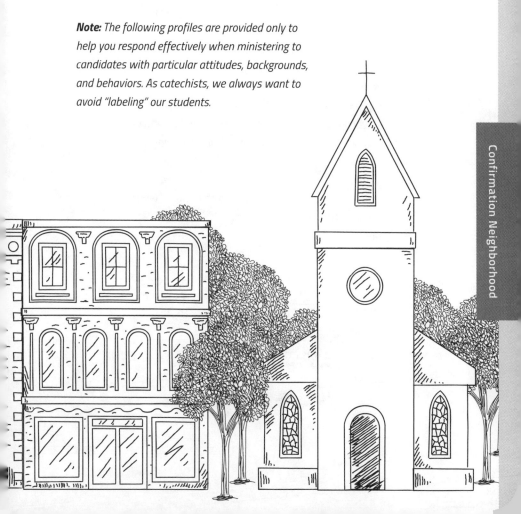

Agnostic or Atheist Candidates

PROFILE

Of the four types of candidates, you will probably only have a few that fall into this category. Somewhere along the way, the agnostic or atheist candidate decided that he did not believe in God or, at least, is highly uncertain of his existence. He is being confirmed only because his parents are forcing him, so you can expect a high level of resistance and perhaps even resentment from him. He might have come to doubt or deny God's existence due to a perceived conflict between science and religion, or maybe he read some books or viewed some YouTube videos by atheists he found convincing, or maybe he just thinks that religious belief in general is superstitious and unenlightened, something that makes no sense in our modern day. He may be in contact with other agnostics or atheists via social media, and this becomes an echo chamber in which belief in God is seen as continuing to believe the world is flat.

TIPS

- Listen respectfully, ask questions, and do not get drawn into an adversarial confrontation.

- Suggest some rational evidence why belief in God actually makes sense.

- Offer some examples of how great saints in our own time—like St. Teresa of Calcutta and St. John Paul II—witness to God's existence and power in the world.

- Do not let your interactions dominate group discussions. Instead, offer to talk one on one when a question or comment is not something helpful for the rest of the group.

- When questions and responses are startling, it is easy to get drawn in and forget that this candidate does not necessarily represent the attitudes and interests of the whole group. Keeping this in mind is very helpful.

- If asked a question you do not know how to answer, be honest—say you are not sure but will find out. Then do so and discuss what you have found out in a future session.

- A candidate's parents may insist that he or she go through Confirmation preparation, but one should not be forced to be confirmed. A candidate needs to have a sincere change of mind and heart by the later stages of the program. Have a heart-to-heart with the parents about this.

Apathetic Candidates

PROFILE

Unlike the agnostic or atheist, the apathetic candidate does not doubt God's existence. He usually believes in God; he just does not really get involved in things (something akin to the philosophy called *deism*). He might say, "So there is a God, and there was a guy named Jesus—but so what? God is 'way out there,' and Jesus lived two thousand years ago. What do they have to offer me? Maybe some guidelines for moral living, but that's about it."

Regarding the Catholic Faith and being confirmed, he might be willing to go through the motions and not rock the boat with his parents. Attending Confirmation prep is the path of least resistance. He will probably avoid sharing or actively participating in the program as much as possible.

TIPS

- Since apathetic candidates often do not see any relevance of the Catholic Faith to their lives (though they might actually believe in some or even most of the major teachings of the Church), make it relevant by finding out what matters to them and connect these things with the Faith.

- Seek to establish a relationship based on honesty and trust. This will go a long way in making them open to what you have to say.

- Encourage their questions and answer them as directly as you can.

- Consider the following: Is their apathy a mask for pain or woundedness? Are they keeping God at a distance because of some major hurts or insecurities? Is there any underlying sense of guilt? Stay tuned, build trust, and ask Jesus to guide your discernment of what your candidates need to hear.

Moderately Invested Candidates

PROFILE

These are the candidates who really do not mind going through Confirmation prep. They may have attended a youth group meeting or volunteered at a parish event or two. They attend Mass regularly and may even be an altar server. While they have participated somewhat in parish life, they have never really made their faith a priority. Their Catholic life is more of an "extracurricular activity" to be fit in between sports, music, friends, etc. That said, these candidates will be fine with coming to your sessions, usually with an openness and a good disposition.

TIPS

- Affirm these candidates' commitment and openness to the process.

- Encourage them to go deeper by asking questions and discussing the issues that confuse or concern them.

- Gently challenge the attitude of having an "extracurricular faith" without diminishing the importance of their other healthy interests and activities.

- Help set the stage for them to have a more direct, powerful encounter with Christ by offering times of prayer, Eucharistic Adoration, and confession.

- Strive to build on the foundation of faith that is already present in their hearts.

Enthusiastic Candidates

PROFILE

Your enthusiastic candidates really want to be there. They have had an encounter with Jesus that has set them on an intentional quest to deepen their faith. They have been on retreats, serve in the parish whenever and wherever possible, and are excited about opportunities to put their faith into action. They are eager to be confirmed.

Since these candidates are *enthusiastic*, they will have a lot to say. They can easily dominate your discussions. With the best of intentions, they may fill any moment of silence with their thoughts. While they are headed in the right direction, they still have much more formation ahead of them.

TIPS

- These candidates truly want to be disciples of Christ, so help them become disciples. Do not be afraid to lead.

- If these candidates begin to dominate your sessions, take them aside, affirm their participation, and ask them to help you to make opportunities for others to share.

- Do not assume that they already know everything about the Faith. Encourage them to learn along with the group.

- Suggest opportunities for additional study, such as a youth Bible study, faith formation program, or youth group. Point them toward solid Catholic books, including the *Catechism of the Catholic Church*.

- Try connecting them with other highly invested young Catholics who share their goal of walking in discipleship.

- Depending on their maturity and social savvy, the other three types of candidates may not be able to relate to the enthusiastic members of your program. You may need to adjust your presentations and discussions with this in mind.

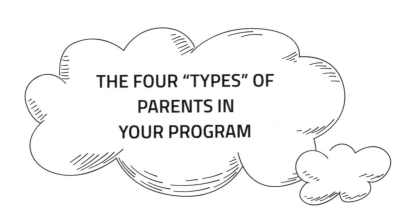

THE FOUR "TYPES" OF PARENTS IN YOUR PROGRAM

Note: *These profiles are presented to offer some insight into what might be happening in the family lives of your candidates. The level of parental involvement in their child's faith formation is the best indicator of a continued practice of the Faith.*

Regardless of how awesome your confirmation program is, the chief catechist in the life of any child is his or her parents. This is the role and responsibility God has given them, starting with the promises they made at their child's baptism. So whatever you can do to better understand, inspire, and equip parents should be prioritized.

Any parent resource that you offer has to be accompanied by an ongoing approach. A book, no matter how good it is, needs a solid lead in, follow up, or small group discussion.

If you do not have an opportunity, understanding is a good place to start. Friendly conversations in the community, whether at church or at the grocery, or even via friendly comments on social media, can get the ball rolling. From there, having a conversation with your team about what can be done at a programmatic level is an effective next step.

PROFILE

These parents have been fairly distant from the regular practice of their Catholic Faith. They attend Mass on Christmas and Easter, and perhaps at weddings and funerals. They may have been raised Catholic, and maybe even attended Catholic school or religious education, but they drifted away from active participation over the years. They may not have been well catechized in the teachings of the Church, or they might simply have gotten caught up in the things of the world and the busyness of life. Then again, they may have been hurt by someone in the Church, feel judged or guilty, or disagree with some of the teachings of the Faith.

Since these parents are "hanging by a sacramental thread," perhaps the son or daughter they have enrolled in your program is as well. Given their limited involvement in the Church, we could ask why they are seeking to have their child confirmed at all. Here are some possibilities:

- They have some vague sense that Confirmation is important, perhaps only as a rite of passage or as "graduation" from religious education.

- They might have some sense that being confirmed will be good for their son or daughter, maybe by connecting them to Jesus and the Church or something like that.

- The candidate's grandparents are really the driving force in faith formation in the family. To appease grandma and grandpa, the parents have agreed to have [name of candidate] confirmed.

- It is their son or daughter who wants to be confirmed.

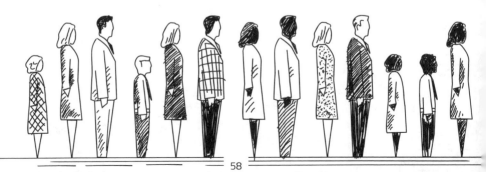

TIPS

- Connecting these parents with the engaging pre-evangelization and evangelization resources now available is a good place to start. Send them links to videos, podcasts, and articles. They might be genuinely surprised by what is out there, and this could begin a deeper conversation.

- Find opportunities to have this conversation, even if it is a friendly message affirming their son or daughter's participation and offering to answer any questions.

- Push for a parent meeting or event that is not about logistics and program details. Set aside time to evangelize.

Extracurricular (Fish Fry and CYO) Parents

PROFILE

These parents attend Mass every Sunday and holy day of obligation. They are involved in parish life, but beyond the parish, their lives are not particularly integrated with the Catholic Faith. They may not have been thoroughly catechized and might be unsure if asked questions about the Faith. Parish life is a priority for them, but in a charitable, social sort of way. These parents may serve on the parish council or in other parish organizations. They are well meaning and upstanding, just not particularly devout. Their formal religious education may have been the last time they considered a deeper vision of the Catholic Faith, but they have stuck faithfully with the Church by investing their time, talent, and treasure.

They are serious about the Confirmation of their children. They might be concerned that their son or daughter seems ambivalent about being confirmed. They are not really sure how to answer tough questions about the Faith because nobody has really equipped them to answer them. They can tell you all about how to run a parish fair or a fish fry, but they are not really sure how to navigate Scripture or the *Catechism*.

TIPS

- Seek out or create opportunities for these parents to learn more about the Faith so that they can share it with their children.

- Invite them into the Confirmation prep process. They might love to coordinate snacks or help with events, and they might get a better sense of what is happening in your program.

- Share Catholic content and invite conversation with them. Coordinate your efforts with the other adult faith formation leaders in your parish.

St. Monica Parents

PROFILE

These are the devout parents; they are "all-in" on their Catholic Faith. Their son or daughter, though, might not be. As a family, they do more than simply attend Mass on Sunday. Together, they might pray the Rosary, say novenas, and celebrate the various feasts of the liturgical calendar, especially those of favorite or patron saints. For some reason, though, their Confirmation candidate son or daughter seems resistant to all this "Church stuff," particularly since they have entered adolescence. This is an understandable cause of worry and frustration for these parents as their child prepares to receive Confirmation. What might be going on here?

- They have been doing a great job in creating a loving and balanced faith environment for their family; their candidate is just in a state of teenage rebellion.

- Without much foundation, their son or daughter perceives them to be rigid, superstitious, and out of touch.

- One parent might be devout, like St. Monica, while the other is much less so in his or her faith (and perhaps does not even attend Mass). This has caused confusion and anxiety for their candidate, which can show itself as rebellion or indifference.

- Some combination of the above.

TIPS

- Be a calming voice. Remind these parents that their love, support, and ongoing practice of the Faith is the best antidote to their child's indifference.

- Listen to them. They are probably open to conversations that could give you clear insight into what is actually going on.

- Offer a clear perspective of the Faith, one that might sound a little different from what they have heard from their parents. Address any question that might arise.

- Share resources—books, videos, podcasts, etc.—with the parents to help start the conversation with their teens.

- If the two parents are in different places in their faith, work with the less devout parent as you would a parent in one of the previously discussed categories. Tread lightly on potential "hot spots," discussing the best course of action with the more devout parent.

Parents on Your Confirmation Team

These are parents who, like all of us, are imperfect in their faith but have something special going on. Their family is united in their devotion to the Catholic Faith. There is ongoing formation in the home, and the candidate, while also imperfect, is striving to live out his or her faith in an authentic way. They can do much in assisting you as you prepare your candidates.

TIPS

- Ask these parents for their prayers and advice.

- Consider having them work with the parents of other candidates in small group discussions or some informal "outreach" calls or meetings.

- Seek to involve them as much as possible. Take time to listen and make sure they feel connected.

Note: *Some parents can actually move between categories from week to week!*

SPONSORS

The role of the sponsor is to assist in a candidate's preparation for Confirmation, certify his or her readiness to be confirmed to the bishop, and serve as a mentor, both before and after reception of the sacrament. The sponsor's important role needs to be made clear from the outset, both to candidates and their parents. It is common for sponsors to be chosen from family members or friends as an honor or because he or she is the candidate's favorite uncle, aunt, or cousin. As a catechist, encourage your candidates to choose a sponsor who can actually fulfill the responsibilities of the role, rather than serving as merely a ceremonial figurehead.

Even if a family member with whom the candidate has little to no relationship is chosen, you can also provide a way for candidates to engage with their sponsors and grow in meaningful connection during the process.

TIPS

- Present the characteristics of a good sponsor during the first meeting of your program.

- Invite a well-chosen sponsor from the previous year's program, along with the person they sponsored, to talk about their experience.

- Assign candidates conversations or activities to do with their sponsors during the preparation process. (If the sponsor is from outside the area, promote conversation via digital means.)

- Consider equipping sponsors with a guide or resource that suggests how they should approach their role.

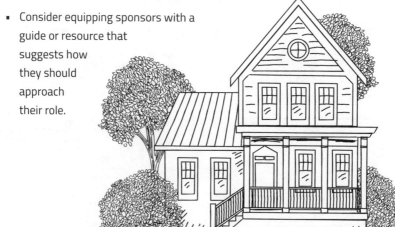

The Art of Confirmation Preparation

PART 1:

STRATEGIES FOR A
SUCCESSFUL PROGRAM

How do I train for my role in Confirmation prep?

Whether you are an experienced, veteran catechist or if you just stepped up to the task for the first time, like Frodo Baggins in *The Lord of the Rings* ("I will take the ring to Mordor, though I do not know the way"), keeping up with today's Confirmation candidate takes some effort. The good news is that sharing the Good News is one of the most important and fulfilling things you can do, and God will give you the grace and strength you need to do it.

To prepare for his big fight, the title character in the movie *Rocky*, like any fighter, began an intensive training program, which culminated in his running up the steps of the Philadelphia Museum of Art. Here are some steps for your training program as a Confirmation catechist:

1. **Pray.** Seriously, this should be obvious, no? To be an effective catechist, you need to cultivate a habit of prayer.

2. **Study.** Commit to learning more about the Faith every day. This could take the form of viewing a short video, reading an article or a paragraph in the *Catechism*, or listening to a podcast. Be sure to do this each day.

3. **Get "culture savvy."** The rapid speed with which our culture is changing affects how your candidates think about and experience everything around them. Study their world so that you can communicate with and understand them more effectively.

4. **Plan.** Take time before each session to prepare, even if the lesson is pre-set for you. Think and pray through what you are about to do.

5. **Assess.** Take time after each session to evaluate what happened so that you are better prepared the next time. If possible, talk things out with others on your team.

How can a shepherd smell more like the sheep?

St. Francis Xavier reportedly made no converts during his first year as a missionary to Asia. What changed? It is no secret. He learned the languages and cultures, spent time with the poor, and lived in the midst of the people with whom he was sharing the gospel. He learned that the shepherd must "smell like the sheep." In other words, as catechists, we need to know the minds, hearts, interests, culture, and quirks of those with whom we want to share the Faith.

In Confirmation preparation, this does not mean using the latest slang and social references (which would come across as phony); it means listening to the candidates and discovering what they care about, with a genuine interest. You do not need to watch the same videos, listen to the same music, or hang out on the same social media platforms as your candidates, but it is helpful to know about what they are watching and doing. It is also helpful to find good things in their world that you can affirm. Find a way into understanding (or at least knowing about) their world, and they will be more open to what you want to share with them.

Here are ten tried-and-true suggestions:

1. Learn their names ... and use them! Make this a priority from the first session.

2. When you take attendance at the beginning of each session, rather than having them reply "Here," ask the candidates to respond with some piece of information that helps you to learn something about each of them. For example, "The last song I listened to was _____" or "The best movie I have seen in the past month was _____" or "The song I listen to when I'm having a bad day is _____." Change the response every session.

3. Ask them how they spend their time.

4. Learn about their social media world, both the good and the bad. Find out what is trendy and influential in their world now, which will likely be different in a few months.

Confirmation Preparation

5. Seek to discover their particular talents and affirm them. If possible, suggest ways that they could use their talents in service to the parish.

6. Show up at a game, play, concert, or event in which a number of them are involved. (Be careful that you do not allow anyone to feel excluded here, though.)

7. When your candidates try to get you off topic, and they will, pay attention to what they are trying to turn the conversation toward. Their topic may not be aligned to the curriculum you planned, but it may reveal an actual interest or question that they have.

8. Have them share the highs and lows of their week. Put on your stethoscope and listen carefully.

9. Ask them what shows they are currently watching. Watch an episode and figure out what is drawing them to it.

10. Find a way to share food and conversation with them. Maybe schedule lunch or dinner before or after a session, maybe a cook-out or a take-out affair.

 ## How can I ensure that I do more listening while my candidates do the talking?

Anyone who has served as a catechist to young people has experienced a group that refuses to talk. To fill in the deafening silence, you talk … and talk … and talk until the session is over. This quickly becomes a pattern. Here are some ways you can break this cycle:

1. Start each session with a **simple icebreaker**. This can be a question-of-the-day, such as, "Where is the best place you have ever eaten?", "Who would you most like to meet?", "What food would you ban forever?", "Do you prefer the beach or the mountains?" etc.

2. If the session hits a wall, do a quick "icebreaker"-like activity to open things up and reduce any tension.

3. When you ask a question and no one responds immediately, wait out the awkward silence. While this might be uncomfortable at first, this sets up the expectation that candidates must participate. Eventually, a question-and-answer rhythm will develop.

4. If candidates are hesitant to answer, ask them to write out simple responses to then share with the group.

5. Affirm everyone who speaks—even if their comments are a bit off. Acknowledge the courage it takes to share in front of one's peers.

6. If a candidate is confrontational or combative about an issue, try to figure out where he or she is coming from. Offer to discuss it further after the session, if necessary.

7. To encourage candidates to engage in discussion, ask open-ended questions that they can understand and can relate to.

8. If a candidate is overly talkative and tends to dominate the group, have an affirming conversation with him and enlist his help in getting others to share.

9. Even affirm candidates who respond with irrelevant platitudes (e.g., "love God," "share with the poor," etc.) to break the awkwardness. Then ask them relevant, relatable follow-up questions.

10. Consider the social dynamics of your group. Are some quiet because they are afraid that the others will judge them? Are some quiet because they are simply shy or introverted? Probably a bit of both. Try to get to know each candidate a bit and you will come to know their needs better. (Do not assume that they aren't talking because they don't like you or because they don't want to be confirmed.)

How can I be a master teacher, like Yoda?

In *Star Wars Episode V: The Empire Strikes Back*, Yoda shows himself to be a great teacher. He does not simply pass on esoteric knowledge or trivial factoids. No, he teaches what is necessary for Luke to actually *become* a Jedi knight. Even if you are not a *Star Wars* fan, there is something to learn from Yoda here—as there is from Mr. Miyagi in the original *Karate Kid* movie or from Mr. Holland in *Mr. Holland's Opus*, both of whom were effective teachers.

What is the point here? In Confirmation prep, many catechists can fall into the trap of thinking that their job is to pass on a bunch of Catholic information to their candidates, forgetting that their primary role is to mentor their students in how to *live* the Faith. Instead of forming Jedi knights, we are forming disciples of Jesus Christ. How, like Yoda, can we be mentors of real discipleship rather than teachers of Catholic facts? Here are a few suggestions:

1. Prepare your candidates to confront real challenges. *(Their own personal Darth Vaders, if you will.)*

2. Remember that you are teaching them to live in the power of the Holy Spirit. *(Even better than the Force, the Holy Spirit is an actual divine Person.)*

3. Move in the gifts of the Holy Spirit yourself so that they can see what it looks like. (*How to lift the X-wing fighter from the swamp, spiritually speaking.)*

4. Go beyond presenting platitudes and describe everyday life as a disciple. *("Never was his mind on where he was ... what he was doing.")*

5. When you ask questions, wait for answers! Do not just feed them the answers when there is an awkward pause. *("Hmmmmm? Hmmmm?")*

6. Challenge them. *("I'm not afraid" ... "You will be.")*

7. Keep in mind that your goal is for them to be disciples. *(Eternally better than being Jedi knights.)*

How do I prepare my candidates for a prayerful Confirmation?

Confirmation is a formal event. Everyone is dressed up. Pictures are taken. People are thinking about what they are supposed to say, where they have to stand, and what they need to do. All of this formality can drive home the dignity, importance, and significance of receiving this sacrament. If we are not careful, though, it can also get in the way of candidates being prayerful, well disposed, and open. In advance of the Confirmation Mass, here are a few things that will help them keep their focus on what is truly important:

1. Spend time walking through the prayers and rite of Confirmation way in advance of the rehearsal. This will make the prayers and signs more familiar and meaningful.

2. Practice their responses and the logistics of the Confirmation rite early and often so it will become familiar to your candidates. This will keep the "nuts-and-bolts" from being a preoccupation or distraction during the ceremony.

3. Make sure your candidates know the "Come, Holy Spirit" prayer, and encourage them to pray it silently throughout the Confirmation Mass.

4. Present each of your candidates with a religious medal, holy card, or sacred object with their Confirmation saint before the ceremony to keep them prayerful and focused.

5. Encourage your candidates to participate in Mass every Sunday. Since Confirmation is received during Mass, going to Mass regularly will help it to feel familiar.

How do I pray for my candidates?

At the risk of stating an obvious platitude, your own prayer life is the most crucial and foundational element in your ministry as a catechist. Remember: Everything you are trying to instill in your candidates is true and good. Your work with them is an extension of the divine plan and mission. You and your candidates are at war with forces that want to see your efforts fail. Cover yourself in prayer—and even throw in some fasting for good measure (see Matthew 17:21).

Here are some thoughts:

1. Step up your daily prayer life with dedicated times.

2. Commit to some specific daily prayer offered for your candidates (e.g., praying a chaplet, the Rosary, or a novena).

3. Pick one candidate to pray for by name every day.

4. Always start and end every session with prayer. (Do not rush through these prayers, which implies that prayer is simply a formality.)

5. Teach your candidates to pray.

 ## How can I make the saints come alive?

Candidates are traditionally encouraged to choose one of the saints for their Confirmation name. Left to their own devices, they might simply pick a name that runs in their family or search for a saint who is the patron of something that interests them. Either is fine—if it is followed by a deeper encounter with their chosen namesake. How can we promote a better process for picking Confirmation names and for introducing candidates to the great cloud of witnesses from Church history? Here are some ways:

1. Spend a brief period each session talking about a particular saint. Do not just read the saint's biography from the Internet or a book; give an overview of his or her life and then offer a comment on something about that saint that personally inspires you.

2. Talk about why you chose your Confirmation name.

3. Have candidates ask their parents and sponsors what names they picked and why.

4. Put resources in your candidates' hands that bring alive the stories of the saints. (Do not have them rely on Wikipedia.)

5. Have them take turns speaking about their chosen name; ask each to present one or two key facts about their saint they found inspiring.

6. Ask sponsors to help their candidate choose their Confirmation name.

 ## How do I strategize to get my candidates to attend Mass?

The current statistics on weekly Mass attendance are pretty abysmal. Many Catholic families are simply not in the pews on Sundays on a regular basis— even though this is a fundamental requirement of our Faith, the bare minimum necessary to follow the third commandment and the precepts of the Church.

Many catechists quickly discover that their confirmation candidates are no exception to sporadic Mass attendance. Unfortunately, this has become the status quo. While the aim of your program goes far beyond this, getting your candidates to come to Mass every Sunday is a step on the road to mature discipleship. How?

1. Make it clear to candidates that Jesus Christ is truly present—body, blood, soul, and divinity—in the Eucharist. At Mass, we do as Jesus commands and share in his body and blood (see Luke 22:19; 1 Corinthians 11:24).

2. Make sure that candidates understand producing inspirational feelings is not the purpose of the Mass. (While these may be pleasant by-products that follow from active participation in the Liturgy, they are not the point.)

3. Present a clear vision of the Mass as the "re-presentation" of the one sacrifice of Christ on the Cross. It is where we bring our works, joys, and sufferings to unite them with Jesus.

4. Encourage candidates to read the Sunday Scripture readings in advance. Tell them that these are available online, so this can be done on their phone or mobile device.

5. Ask your candidates to consider helping at Mass in some capacity, perhaps as altar servers, lectors, ushers, or greeters.

6. Encourage candidates to attend Mass together, for example before or after a Confirmation prep session or service project.

How can I make confession less scary?

"Bless me, Father, for I have sinned. It has been ... ummm ... a long time ... since my last confession."

Aside from attending Mass on Sundays and holy days of obligation, celebrating the sacrament of Reconciliation is the most important ongoing sacramental practice for a Catholic. We all need the forgiveness and healing that come from this beautiful gift. For varying reasons, however, regular confession has become uncommon, even among weekly Mass attendees. Your candidates might be scared, embarrassed, or otherwise not interested in going to confession. It is even possible that it has been years since their last confession. Encouraging, teaching, modeling, and mentoring are crucial here. Establishing the habit during Confirmation preparation could be a life-altering change. Who knows what benefits of regular confession could mean for the future of your candidates. Here are some ideas:

1. Do not assume that every candidate remembers how to go to confession. Walk them through the rite of Penance, step-by-step, to reassure them.

2. Drive home that the sacrament of Reconciliation is about just that—*reconciliation*. It is about healing. Spend some time discussing what reconciliation means and why everyone needs to be reconciled to God and others.

3. Since your candidates might be nervous, equip them with resources that calm their nerves. For example, there are several apps with examinations of conscience, the order of the sacrament of Reconciliation, and the act of contrition.

4. Speak about your own experiences with this powerful sacrament.

5. Ask your pastor to have a penance service for your candidates. Consider inviting their sponsors and parents, as well.

How do I build a great strategy for technology?

Your candidates were born in the digital age. None of them remember a time before the Internet, social media, and streaming video and music. Most spend hours every day looking at screens. They are deeply tied into this virtual world, socially, psychologically, and emotionally—even academically. They are hooked. In one way or another, all of us are hooked.

This new digital world and its associated technology has opened up some great opportunities for evangelization and catechesis. We can share up-to-date videos, access daily readings, and even survey and quiz students with devices that they literally have in their pockets. Of course, these devices tend to get in the way of real engagement and interaction—and candidates can quickly zone out. So do we have them keep their phones off (or turned in) or find a way to use them efficiently in our Confirmation prep efforts? Here are some things to consider:

1. Do not be too "anti-technology" with your candidates. If you decide, though, that you do not want them to use any devices and ask them to keep them off (or even turn them in for the session), be sure to offer a compelling reason why.

2. If you decide to utilize technology, keep it limited to specific things that candidates can do with their phones. For example, look up the Mass reading for that day, view a short video that ties in with the session topic, or research the life of a saint, perhaps one they can choose as their Confirmation name.

3. As a model to candidates, limit your own smartphone use during a session. For example, do not reply to texts or answer a call, unless particularly urgent.

4. Become familiar with their digital world. Ask them what apps they use regularly.

5. Talk to your candidates about the need for "digital purity" and the dangers of pornography.

6. Talk to them about being safe online.

7. Coordinate and communicate with parents about numbers five and six.

Note: *Part 3 of this section presents some in-depth tips on using technology in your Confirmation preparation efforts.*

PART 2:

CLASSROOM MANAGEMENT

What if my group is constantly on their phones?

Establish a device/smartphone policy from the start and stick to it. You might have a basket for candidates to turn in their devices at the start of each session, or set a rule that you will confiscate any devices that are used during the session. You might even allow some limited use for more mature candidates and only address "problem" behaviors. The important thing is to set norms at the beginning and adhere to them consistently.

What if my group keeps going off on tangents during discussions?

Slaying the "tangent monster" is an important task for a catechist. Do not get frustrated and take the oxygen out of the room. The fact that candidates are comfortable enough to talk about *anything* is a step in the right direction. Sidetracked discussions can also give you a good idea of what your candidates care about and what they think—and can help break the ice. Patiently and gently redirect the discussion back to the topic at hand. If possible, point the tangential point back to the actual content being discussed.

What if nobody says anything?

If you just read about tangents and think, "I wish," you might have some experience with a group where nobody says anything. This could have to do with how comfortable your candidates are with one another. It might be that there is a particular candidate (or a few) that the other candidates find intimidating. Try to diagnose the source of your group's silence and strive to build up their comfort level. It might help to start with the same questions or to provide alternate ways to respond, e.g., having them write their responses in a notebook and then discuss them. Ask for a show of hands as a way of answering a question.

How do I handle a candidate (or candidates) with serious behavior problems?

- Avoid being drawn into an adversarial role.

- Avoid rewarding attention-seeking behavior with too much attention.

- Stay calm and be firm in your response.

- Show interest in and concern for the candidates who are misbehaving.

- Seek to have a conversation with the problem candidate(s) outside of the group.

- Try to find out the source of the bad behavior. This might be as simple as asking. In other cases, you may discover what is going on as the program progresses.

How do I handle a candidate who expresses that they don't believe in God or who has issues with being confirmed?

- Do not be shocked. Be supportive and invite them to share their thoughts—without derailing the topic.

- Listen carefully to what the candidate is sharing and seek to address it later, outside of the group setting.

- If appropriate, seek to involve the candidate's sponsor.

- Have a conversation with the candidate's parents. There needs to be direct support and conversation with the candidate at home on his or her issues.

- If the candidate comes toward the end of the program and is still having issues with being confirmed, you will need to meet with the parents and the candidate to discuss whether he or she should be confirmed. As mentioned, a candidate needs to be properly disposed to receive this sacrament (or any sacrament).

PART 3:

TIPS FOR USING TECHNOLOGY— WHEN CONFIRMATION GOES DIGITAL

It goes without saying that face-to-face learning and formation is preferable, but circumstances may sometimes require you to have remote sessions via technology. The good news is that we now have the digital resources to make remote catechesis and interaction possible.

Depending on the circumstances and geography of your parish, you might even choose to build some remote sessions into your regular Confirmation prep schedule. For example, if the territory of your parish is unusually large, this might be done to lighten the load on parents from bringing their teens to multiple events at some distance from one another. You might even schedule a remote session for sponsors who live out of the area.

Since distance learning is a new reality for Confirmation prep, it is worth covering our bases and considering some best practices.

Confirmation Preparation

How do I best consider the tech needs and capabilities of my candidates?

- Meet with your pastor and other members of your parish team to determine a technology plan for your Confirmation preparation program.

- Present your technology plan to the candidates and parents before your first session. Discuss how it will be implemented in case of interruptions to your calendar.

- Include FAQs about your technology plan and requirement during the registration process.

- Include a technology policy, in line with your diocese's safe environment protocols, with registration materials.

- For any candidates that have limited (or no) Internet access, make sure that printed copies of any needed materials are available. ***Note:*** *Most video conference apps allow for remote use with a smartphone using cellular data.*

- Develop a plan for any unscheduled remote sessions, due to weather or some other event.

 ## What are some best practices for remote video sessions?

- Do what you can to make the session fun and inviting—an *event.* Make sure you present from an appropriate location (i.e., a home office or parish meeting room), with an appealing background and sufficient lighting. Consider having some music playing quietly in the background, if it doesn't interfere with the discussion.

- Ask candidates to find a spot in their home that is conducive to focusing and having a conversation. Tell them to avoid common areas or high traffic spots of their house.

- Remind candidates to wear appropriate attire when appearing on camera.

- Most video conferencing platforms give you controls as the leader (organizer) of your meeting. Utilize your tools as leader to control the audio and video, admit participants, and even remove a participant from a session, if necessary.

- Be sure to follow all safe environment protocols established by your diocese. Enable a waiting room so that you control who is admitted. If your app allows it, record the session. These strategies can be an added layer of protection.

 ## What is the best way to pray remotely?

- Ask your candidates to share their prayer intentions using the chat feature. Everyone can then see them and offer them when you pray.

- Call your group to prayer at the start of the session. Ask for cameras on, microphones muted, and distractions to go away. You will be able to see when everyone is ready.

- Have a prayer schedule where candidates can sign up to lead the prayer. A decade of the Rosary, with individual candidates leading the Our Father, Hail Marys, and Glory Be, can work particularly well in a video conference.

- Consider using the *lectio divina* approach. Read a passage from Scripture, then go around and ask each candidate to comment on one word or phrase that stood out to them. Then, invite candidates to share their thoughts on the meaning of the verses.

 ## How can I present well remotely?

Whether you are introducing something the candidates will watch, kicking off a discussion, or teaching a lesson, here are a few tips:

- Balance screen sharing with eye contact.

- Smile often and remember to look into the camera.

- Address candidates by name.
- If talking for an extended period, ask candidates to offer their feedback in the chat feature. This helps them stay tuned in and participate. Asking candidates something subjective that supports your point will help them stay tuned in.

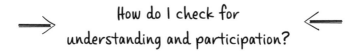

How do I check for understanding and participation?

- The chat feature allows for quick and fluid check-in. Pause until all have had a chance to respond.
- In advance, create a quick assessment to check for understanding and privately collect questions. Consider using Google Forms or even a simple email for this.

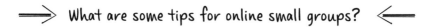

What are some tips for online small groups?

- Call on candidates one at a time.
- Allow more introverted candidates to type answers in chat.
- Interact with strong affirmation just as you would face to face.
- Ask candidates to turn their cameras on during conversation if possible.

Conclusion

Your field guide experience now just needs a field test. In this *Catechist's Field Guide to Confirmation*, we have considered quite a few things. Perfection, of course, is not the goal; creating and running an effective program is. You may encounter situations that we have not discussed here, or even anticipated. Make a habit out of praying the "Come, Holy Spirit" prayer. If you have a moment of concern or doubt and think, "Wait, what did the field guide say about this?" or "Wait, this candidate does not fit any of the profiles. What do I do?!" ... stop ... take a breath. Pray to the Holy Spirit. Remember that you were confirmed and that all of the Spirit's gifts and fruits you read about here are within you. Be confident and bold in the Spirit within you ... you've got this!

Come, Holy Spirit, fill the hearts of your faithful and kindle in them the fire of your love. Send forth your Spirit and they shall be created. And you shall renew the face of the earth.

AMEN.

ADDITIONAL RESOURCES

ASCENSION PRESENTS

Ascension Presents is your home for free Catholic media to keep you going throughout the week. Find videos, podcasts, and blog posts from people like Fr. Mike Schmitz, Fr. Josh Johnson, Danielle Bean, Jeff Cavins, and many others! *ascensionpresents.com*

THE SACRED THAT SURROUNDS US: HOW EVERYTHING IN A CATHOLIC CHURCH POINTS TO HEAVEN

by Andrea Zachman

The Sacred That Surrounds Us is a beautiful, high-quality book that shows and tells the truth of thousands of years of Catholic tradition. HD photography reveals the beauty of objects found in every Catholic church, and clear, thorough descriptions bring them to life.

Each description includes historical facts, a discussion of symbolism, and often a quote from the Church Fathers or the Bible about the item. This book helps Catholics transform every visit to a Catholic church, no matter how plain, into a prayerful journey of faith by discovering the sacred that surrounds them.

THE GREAT ADVENTURE CATHOLIC BIBLE

Every Catholic needs this Bible! *The Great Adventure Catholic Bible* makes the complexity of reading the Bible simple.

The narrative approach gives the big picture of salvation history and shows how everything ties together. This is the only Bible that incorporates *The Great Adventure's* color-coded *Bible Timeline*™ Learning System, a system that has made *The Great Adventure* the most popular and influential Bible study program in the English-speaking world. The color-coded tools make it easy to read and easy to remember.

Truly a "game changer"! There has never been another Bible like it.

CHOSEN: YOUR JOURNEY TOWARD CONFIRMATION

by Chris Stefanick, Ron Bolster, and Colin & Aimee MacIver

Chosen takes young people on a journey through the entire Catholic Faith in all its richness and vitality. Teens will be captivated by the story, from Creation all the way through salvation history, and they will come to see how the sacraments, prayer, and discipleship are the keys to a happy life. The goal of this 24-lesson program is nothing short of winning over the hearts of teens and making them disciples of Christ.

notes

notes

notes